Spot 7

Toys

By KIDSLABEL

chronicle books · san francisco

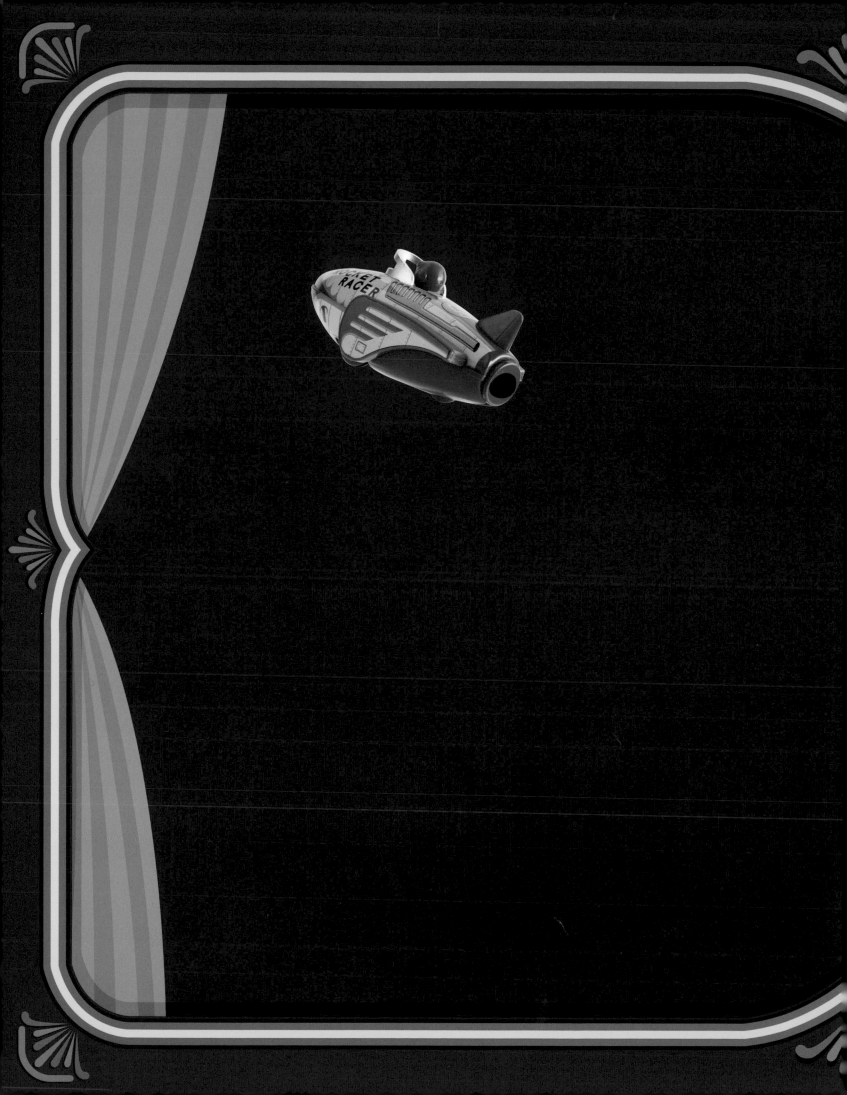

The pairs of photos in this book of picture riddles seem the same...

but look carefully.
There are 7 differences.

You'll also find a **riddle** below each pair of photos.
Need a **clue**? The answer is always something
in the picture above.

Extra Challenge
Looking only at the right-hand pages (and don't forget
the front cover!), find:

7 **rocking horses**
5 **keys**
4 **airplanes**
2 **watering cans**
2 **windmills**
2 **pocket watches**

and a **slice of cake.**

It will wait for the bus in bad weather.
It stands so that others may sit.
But when the bus nears,
it's patently clear:
It couldn't get on; it won't fit!

I can snap without fingers.
I can swim without fins.
I'll play hide and seek before I eat,
but you'd better watch out if I win!

As fast as the wind
four runners race each other,
but not one can win.

My first is five to Romans,
my second and fifth are one,
my fourth's as much as fifty,
and the rest are half of none.

```
  6  faces
 21  eyes
+ 8  corners
─────
  1  ─────
```

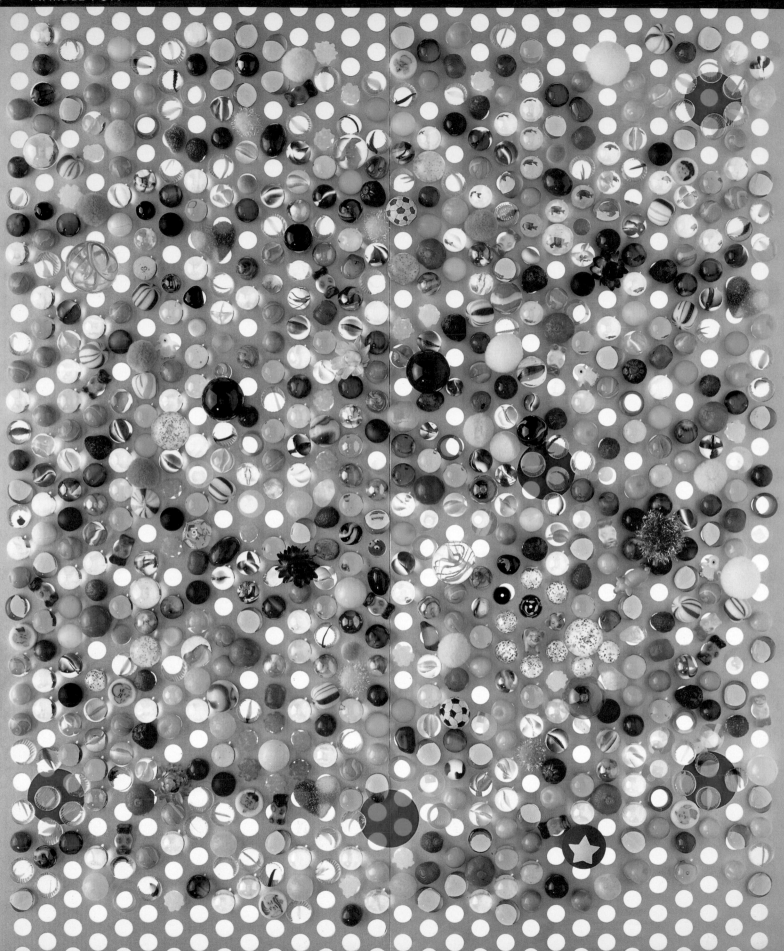

These little sweeties are dressed in red,
freckled with dots, and on their heads
are little caps of frilly green.
How many of them can be seen?

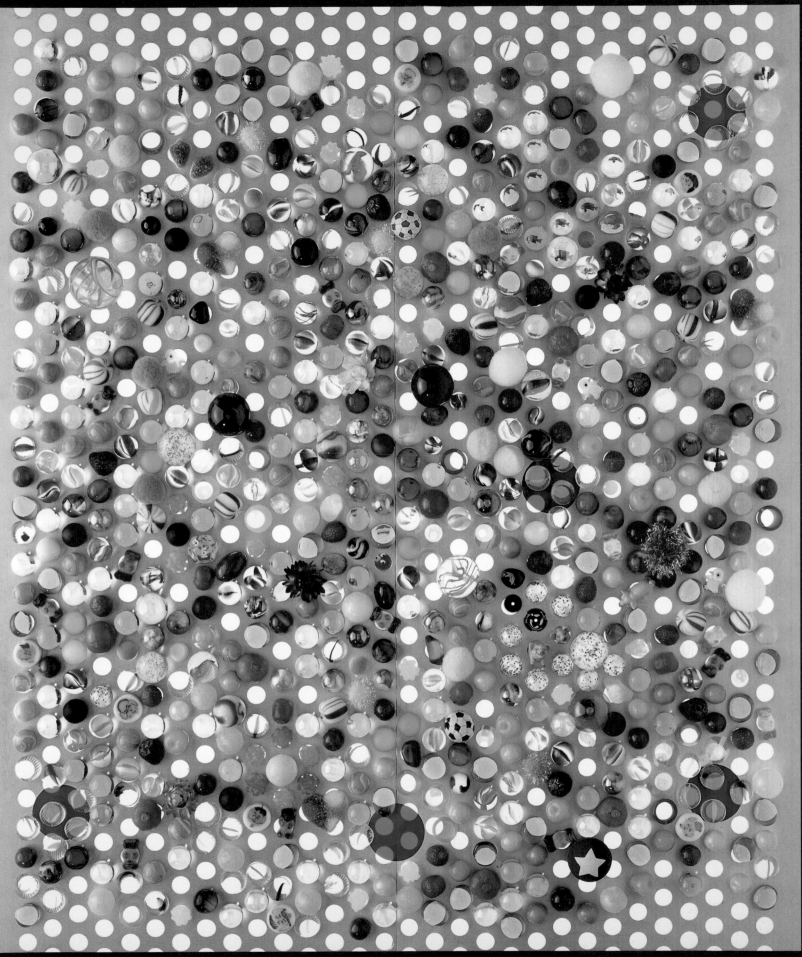

In a house with beds of straw
came a hungry thief.
The crime was over easily,
but no cause for grief—

home the burglar scrambled
to coffee in his cup
and breakfast on the table:
sunny-side up.

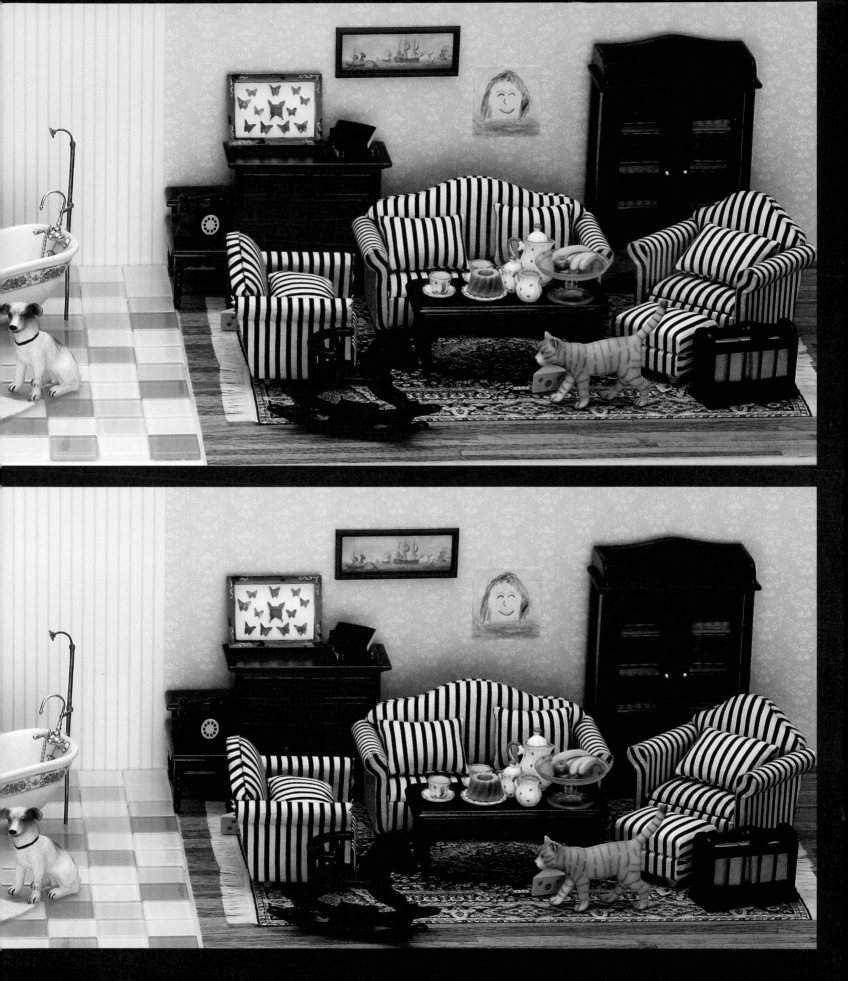

My first is in keep but not castle,
my second's in rich but not plush,
my third is in crown but not scepter,
my fourth is in straight but not flush.

Dolls' apartment

What visits flowers like a bee?
What has a head but cannot see?
And, like a storm cloud with a spout,
tips to let its rain come out?

Dolls' apartment

A riddle for two voices:
The universe

is primarily composed of this
never mind

an atom
is primarily composed of this
never mind

the stars

the spinning
planets

the occasional
asteroid

Though you cannot see it
you can know it by the dark.

They say a stitch in time saves nine,
but that's way off base. I have 216 stitches,
but I see as many walked or out as any I'd call safe.

Those who use me make notes (though I'm no pencil).
Those who use me keep time (though I'm no clock).
Pedal me hard, I won't travel.
With all of my keys, I've no lock.

Front and Back Covers: Look for

a key
a letter **m**
a ball near a dollar sign
a ball near a sunflower
a blue stone by a bottle
a blue star by a heart
a faint light by a fish's fin

You, Robot: Look for

a bird on a roof
a robot in a window
a fence on the far left
a newspaper
a bus-stop sign
a robot crossing the street
a paving stone

Around the Bed in 80 Days: Look for

a hot air balloon
an astronaut's flag
a pile of coffee beans
three dolls in a row
a camel
an extra penguin
a row of blue fishes

The Bridges of Maze County: Look for

an extra yellow duck
an orange fish
a white rat near a ghost
a red and green present
a spoon between a nest and a book
a sheep on the left
a green stone near a purple gem

The Sturdy Nine Steps: Look for

a fish tank
a sun
a face in a car
a beak near a fish
a porcelain mask
a gramophone handle
a blue bead on a green bed

A Suitable Toy: Look for

a card at the top left
a yellow bead with a face
two sumo wrestlers
a card at the top center
a clear glass bead by a paper crane
a paper star near a paper crane
a pink ring by a yellow ring

Marble Fun: Look for

two little red things near a fuzzy
    yellow thing
an orange and red heart
a yellow marble beneath the heart
a yellow die near a red flower
a black gear on a white light
a blue ball with a star
a white marble between a red marble,
    a yellow marble, and a green marble

Cat, Dog, and Mouse: Look for

an extra pancake
a spatula
a mouse on the floor
a mouse in a mirror
a toothbrush
a roll of toilet paper
a striped pillow

Chances Are: Look for

a card over a jack
a coin by some cards
a die at the top of the square of dice
a figure in the middle of the square of dice
a figure near the bottom-left corner of the
   square
a cane's handle
a die near a lion

An Apartment of One's Own: Look for

a darker roof tile
a little guy attached to a balloon
an apple on a refrigerator
a little man near a clock
a cat's tail
a bear by a duck
a monkey on TV

A Brave New Asteroid: Look for

a pink stone near the top
a blue marble near an orange alien
a stone near a green alien on the right
a green alien *and*
the astronaut he's next to
a space shuttle on the left
a stone on a green asteroid

The Art of Memory: Look for

a little man with a flag near a robot
a robot's head
a kitten in a mug
something near a rocking horse
an extra star near a bird
a merry-go-round
a red die near a green die

A March to the Music of Time: Look for

a monkey's tongue
a gramophone
a chair near a piano
a blue block behind a nutcracker
a violin behind a nutcracker
a book on the right
an arm near a cow

Answers to the Riddles:

You, Robot: bench
Around the Bed in 80 Days: alligator
The Bridges of Maze County: windmill
The Sturdy Nine Steps: violin
A Suitable Toy: die
Marble Fun: strawberry
Cat, Dog, and Mouse: egg
Chances Are: king
An Apartment of One's Own: watering can
A Brave New Asteroid: space
The Art of Memory: baseball
A March to the Music of Time: piano

Still can't find them? Look at our Web page!

http://www.chroniclebooks.com/spot7

Spot some more! fun in

available wherever books are sold!

I love feathers best when still attached;
I love to bathe, but dislike wet;
I like to play with my food.
I *hate* the vet.

First published in the United States in 2008 by Chronicle Books LLC.

Copyright © 2003, 2005, 2006, 2007 by KIDSLABEL.
English text © 2008 by Chronicle Books LLC.
Originally published in Japan in 2003, 2005, 2006, 2007 under the titles *Doko Doko? Seven 1*;
Doko Doko? Seven 6 Dream; *Doko Doko? Seven 7 World*; and *Doko Doko? Seven 8 Treasure* by
KIDSLABEL Corp.
English translation rights arranged with KIDSLABEL Corp. through Japan Foreign-Rights Centre.
All rights reserved.

English type design by Eloise Leigh.
Typeset in Super Grotesk and Trade Gothic.
Manufactured in China.

Library of Congress Cataloging-in-Publication Data
KIDSLABEL.
Spot 7 Toys / by KIDSLABEL.
    p. cm. — (Spot 7)
 ISBN 978-0-8118-6563-0
 1. Toys—Juvenile literature. 2. Picture puzzles—Juvenile literature. I. KIDSLABEL. II. Title. III. Series.
 GV1218.5.T69 2008
 790.1'33—dc22
 2008005281

10 9 8 7 6 5 4 3 2

Chronicle Books LLC
680 Second Street, San Francisco, California 94107

www.chroniclekids.com